CELEBRATIONS AROUND THE WORLD

ILLUSTRATED BY KATY HALFORD

Illustrated by Katy Halford

Created and designed for DK by Plum5 Ltd

Editor Sophie Parkes
US Editor Liz Searcy
Editorial Assistant Katie Lawrence
Managing Art Editor Gemma Glover
Design Assistant Brandie Tully-Scott
Senior Producer, Preproduction Tony Phipps
Senior Producer Amy Knight
Jacket Coordinator Issy Walsh
Creative Technical Support Sonia Charbonnier
Creative Director Helen Senior
Publishing Director Sarah Larter
Consultants Alasdair Richardson and Rhiannon Love

First American Edition, 2019
Published in the United States by DK Publishing
1450 Broadway, Suite 801, New York, NY 10018

Copyright © 2019 Dorling Kindersley Limited DK,
a Division of Penguin Random House LLC
22 23 10 9 8 7 6 5 4 3
007–314063–Aug/2019

A catalog record for this book is available from
the Library of Congress.
ISBN: 978-1-4654-8390-4

DK books are available at special discounts when purchased in
bulk for sales promotions, premiums, fund-raising, or educational
use. For details, contact: DK Publishing Special Markets, 1450
Broadway, Suite 801, New York, NY 10018 SpecialSales@dk.com

Printed in China

A WORLD OF IDEAS:
SEE ALL THERE IS TO KNOW

www.dk.com

CONTENTS

NEW YEAR

On December 31, people in many countries around the world gather together to celebrate the last day of the old year and the arrival of a new one. As the clock strikes midnight, they exchange hugs and good wishes. Big cities such as London, Berlin, and Sydney host spectacular firework displays.

Various customs are believed to bring luck in the New Year. In Denmark, people smash plates on their friends' doors to show their love, while in South America, they wear yellow underwear for luck. In Spain, people eat 12 grapes at midnight—one with each chime of the clock.

In Scotland, New Year's Eve is called Hogmanay. The Scottish song "Auld Lang Syne", which celebrates friendship, is sung at midnight. A tradition called "first footing" claims that the first visitor of the year to a home will bring good luck, as long as they bring a gift such as shortbread or some coal for the fire.

The Japanese New Year festival is called *Shogatsu*. People clean their homes and decorate them with ornaments and pine, plum, and bamboo branches. They visit temples and shrines to pray. At midnight, bells in the temples are rung to welcome the New Year.

CHINESE NEW YEAR

Also known as the Spring Festival, Chinese New Year is one of the most important Chinese holidays. It is celebrated in many countries. Before the festival, people clean their homes to get rid of any bad luck and to start the New Year afresh.

Families enjoy a special meal together. They eat dishes such as fish and dumplings to bring them wealth in the New Year. Noodles symbolize happiness and a long life, and oranges are thought to bring good luck. Children are given red gifts, such as envelopes containing money.

In Chinese legend, every New Year a monster called Nian came to villages to hunt for food. The villagers learned that he was afraid of fire, noise, and the color red. Today, people decorate their homes with red lanterns and light noisy firecrackers to scare Nian away.

In cities around the world, there are colorful parades of acrobats, jugglers, dancers, and musicians. Traditional Chinese lion or dragon dances are performed to bring luck for the year ahead. The celebrations end with huge firework displays.

KITE FESTIVALS

Kite festivals are held all over the world, from Bondi Beach in Australia, to Washington State in the United States. The skies are filled with hundreds of kites of all shapes and sizes. There are simple, diamond-shaped kites, box kites, moon-shaped kites, flying-dragon kites, and many more.

At the Sagami Giant Kite Festival in Japan, some of the largest kites in the world take to the air. The colorful kites are made out of bamboo and paper. It can take teams of as many as one hundred people to lift one kite off the ground.

In Italy, the Cervia International Kite Festival is held each year on a huge, sandy beach. Hundreds of kite artists perform acrobatic flights and show off their beautiful kites. Kite experts teach children how to make and fly their own kites.

The International Kite Festival in the state of Gujarat in India is part of the celebration of Uttarayan. This marks the day when winter begins to turn into summer, and the gods are said to wake up from their winter sleep. People fly kites from rooftops, and kite shops stay open all night.

RIO CARNIVAL

This celebration, held in Rio de Janeiro in Brazil, is one of many festivals in the world that takes place just before Lent—a time when Christians prepare for Easter by giving up rich foods, such as meat or sweets.

The Rio Carnival is one of the biggest and most spectacular festivals in the world. It lasts for several days and is a huge celebration filled with dancing, parades, and music. Millions of people come to the city of Rio de Janeiro to enjoy the entertainment.

To start the Carnival celebrations, the Mayor of Rio de Janeiro gives the key to the city to a man dressed as King Momo, the mischievous king of Carnival. When Momo starts dancing, the fun begins. Across the city, there are street parties, concerts, and costume balls.

The highlight of Rio Carnival is the samba parade, in which samba schools compete with each other. Samba is an African-Brazilian dance style. Huge teams of musicians, artists, fashion designers, and dancers work hard all year to prepare for the festival.

LAS FALLAS

The spring festival of Las Fallas is celebrated each March in the city of Valencia in Spain. The townspeople set up hundreds of giant sculptures, or *fallas*, each telling a different story. The *fallas* are decorated with puppets, called *ninots*, made of wood and papier-mâché (a mixture of paper and glue).

People walk around admiring the *fallas* and enjoying street foods, such as tapas, sausages, and paella. Sweet treats include fried dough sticks called *churros* and pumpkin fritters called *buñuelos de calabaza*. Both are delicious dipped in hot chocolate!

For three days, the streets of Valencia are full of music, fireworks, and partying. People dress up in traditional costumes and take part in parades. There are firework displays and dazzling light shows every day, and streets are lit up by thousands of lightbulbs.

On the last day of the festival, the *fallas* are judged, and the winning *ninot* is shown in the local museum. The festival ends with a spectacular fire parade of rockets, flames, and smoke. At midnight, all the *fallas* are loaded with firecrackers and burned.

HOLI

Holi is a Hindu festival that takes place in spring. It is celebrated in India, Nepal, and many other countries. It is sometimes known as the Festival of Colors. Holi lasts for one night and one day and celebrates spring, friendship, family, and the victory of good over evil.

Holi celebrations begin in the evening, when bonfires are lit to symbolize the defeat of the wicked Holika. In Hindu legend, she tried to harm her nephew when he refused to worship the evil king Hiranyakashipu. People gather around the bonfires to pray and perform Hindu traditions.

On the day of Holi, there is a huge paint fight! People throw colored powders called *gulal* at each other and splash people with colored water from water jets and balloons. Everyone joins in, young or old. There is dancing, singing, and traditional drum music.

In the evening, people clean up and put on fresh clothes. They visit friends and family to exchange greetings, gifts, and special Holi sweets. They forgive old offenses and enjoy spending time together.

EASTER

Christians celebrate Easter Sunday, the day that Jesus Christ, who they believe to be the Son of God, rose from the dead. Easter is also connected to the arrival of spring and new life. Eggs are a common symbol of Easter because they bring new life into the world.

Legend has it that a friendly rabbit, known as the Easter Bunny, brings chocolate eggs and gifts to children. On Easter morning, children hunt for eggs hidden around their homes and gardens. Hard-boiled eggs are decorated or rolled down hills in races.

Many children decorate hats, called Easter bonnets, with items such as eggs, chicks, or rabbits. They show them off at Easter parades. However, it's not always about eggs. In Sweden, children dress up as witches and visit houses asking for candy.

Roast lamb is a popular meal around the world on Easter Sunday. Christians in Ethiopia often celebrate Easter, which they call *Fasika*, with a chicken stew. Many Europeans eat traditional Easter breads, and in Jamaica they enjoy special spiced buns with cheese.

MAY DAY

On May 1, known as May Day, people celebrate the beginning of summer. Many festivals throughout history have celebrated this time of year, such as the Roman festival for Flora, the goddess of flowers and fruits, and the Celtic festival of Beltane.

In northern Europe, the evening before May Day is called Walpurgis Night. In German legend, witches gather in the mountains on this evening, so bonfires are lit to scare them away. In Finland, people have parties and enjoy a special spiced drink called sima.

May Day celebrations often include a maypole—a tall pole that is stuck in the ground with brightly colored ribbons tied to the top. The ribbons are held by dancers who weave in and out, creating a pattern as they go.

In Britain, May Day parades are led by a newly crowned May queen. They may also feature Jack-in-the-Green, a mischievous character painted green and draped in plants. English morris dancers perform traditional dances with bells tied to their legs. They wave colorful handkerchiefs and knock sticks together in time to the music.

EID AL-FITR

Eid al-Fitr marks the end of Ramadan, which is a holy month in the Islamic calendar. During Ramadan, Muslims are not allowed to eat or drink between sunrise and sunset. This is known as fasting, which is one of the things that Muslims do to live a good life.

Eid begins at sunset. As soon as the moon is spotted in the sky, Muslims put on new clothes and pray at the mosque or at outdoor services. Some decorate their hands with beautiful patterns using a special dye called henna.

Celebrations go on for as many as three days. The most important event is a special feast that is shared with neighbors, friends, and family. People wish each other a happy holiday, exchange cards and gifts, and give money to those in need.

In Turkey, Eid al-Fitr is also known as the Sugar Feast, or Şeker Bayramı, because desserts such as baklava and Turkish delight are enjoyed during this time. Children go from door to door wishing their neighbors a happy Bayram and are given sweets in return.

MIDSUMMER

People celebrate the longest day of the year in a festival called Midsummer, also known as the summer solstice. For many Christians, Midsummer is also the time to celebrate the Feast of Saint John the Baptist. Saint John was a religious teacher who told people about Jesus Christ.

In Sweden, Midsummer is one of the most important holidays of the year. People gather to watch traditional dancing around a flower-covered pole. They enjoy a special feast of dishes such as pickled herring, salmon, and strawberries.

Many Scandinavian countries celebrate Midsummer with picnics and parties held around huge bonfires. In countries such as Denmark and Norway, models of witches may be burned on the bonfires. People sometimes jump over the fires because they believe this will bring them wealth and luck.

Midsummer is believed to be a time of magic. In many places, it is the best time to pick herbs for potions or medicines. In Icelandic legend, cows talk and seals turn into humans at Midsummer. It is also thought to be lucky to roll around in wet grass with no clothes on!

FOURTH OF JULY

The Fourth of July is one of the biggest national holidays in the United States. It marks the day when the US became independent. On this day in 1776, the Americans announced that they were no longer part of the British Empire and would rule themselves from then on.

The independence of the United States is celebrated across the country. At noon, soldiers on army bases fire the "salute to the union"—50 gunshots fired to represent the 50 states that make up the United States.

Americans spend the day having picnics, barbecues, and parties, or watching sports on TV. It is estimated that more than 150 million hot dogs are eaten on the Fourth of July! People dress up in red, white, and blue, and American flags are seen everywhere.

There are parades of people dressed in historical costumes. The parades have marching bands that play "The Star-Spangled Banner," the national anthem of the United States. In the evening, famous landmarks and buildings are lit up, and there are huge firework displays.

BASTILLE DAY

More than 200 years ago, the people of France were suffering under the rule of King Louis XVI. They had to give the king some of their money as taxes, and there was not enough food to go around. People who protested against the king were sent to prisons, including the fearsome Bastille fortress in Paris.

On July 14, 1789, an angry crowd attacked the Bastille fortress to set the prisoners free. The revolution that followed forced the king off the throne and created the modern Republic of France.

July 14 became known as Bastille Day and was
declared a national holiday in France in 1880.
It has been celebrated each year ever since. People
spend the day with family and friends and attend
parties or concerts.

A huge military parade is held each year on the Champs-
Élysées avenue in Paris. Thousands of soldiers, the police,
and the Paris fire department take part. Massive tanks roll
down the avenue, and army planes fly overhead. The French
president starts the parade and inspects the soldiers.

VENICE REGATTA

The Venice Regatta is a festival of boat races. It takes place in September on the Canal Grande, one of the main canals in the Italian city of Venice. It is an opportunity for Venetian gondoliers to show off their rowing skills in long, narrow boats called gondolas.

The event begins with a parade of 16th-century-style boats, rowed by gondoliers in traditional costumes. At the front is a splendid ship that is painted gold, which carries people dressed as the Doge (Duke) of Venice, his wife, and other important officials from a long time ago.

A ceremony is held at the Santa Maria della Salute Church to bless the competitors and their boats. The teams competing in the regatta are also introduced to each other here. Spectators gather along the shore and on floating stands in the canal to watch the races.

The races begin! They are conducted in traditional gondolas. The boats are brightly colored, so it's easy to see who is winning. Rowers compete for *bandieri* (flags). These are red for first place, white for second, and green for third.

ROSH HASHANAH AND YOM KIPPUR

Rosh Hashanah is the Jewish New Year and celebrates what Jews believe was the creation of the world. It is an opportunity for people to reflect on their behavior and say sorry for things they have done wrong in the past year. Jews believe that God will judge them ten days later at Yom Kippur, the holiest day in the Jewish calendar.

A trumpet made of a ram's horn, called a *shofar*, is blown to mark the start of Rosh Hashanah. Jews visit the synagogue and spend time with their families. A candlelit feast with special food is enjoyed, during which prayers and blessings are made.

Apples dipped in honey represent the hope that sweet things will happen in the coming year, and a round loaf of *challah* bread represents the circle of life. Pomegranates symbolize a year ahead full of good deeds, just as the pomegranate is full of seeds.

Ten days later, during Yom Kippur, people ask forgiveness for any bad things they have done. They spend the day praying, often in the synagogue. They do not eat or drink for 25 hours. The end of the festival is marked with a blast of the *shofar*, followed by a feast.

MID-AUTUMN FESTIVAL

Also known as the Moon or Harvest Moon Festival, the Mid-Autumn Festival is celebrated in China, Vietnam, and other Asian countries. It occurs in fall, when the bright full moon is in the sky. Families gather together to enjoy each other's company and to give thanks for a good harvest.

People come out at night to look at the moon, which is a symbol of peace and friendship. In Chinese legend, the goddess Chang'e flew to the moon after drinking a special potion that let her live forever. She is said to still be there, along with her friend the Jade Rabbit, a popular character of the festival.

Decorated mooncakes are a central part of the festival and are offered to Chang'e to make sure the harvest is good. They are made of sweet pastry and are usually filled with red bean or date paste and ingredients such as salted egg yolk, fruit, and nuts.

Beautiful colored lanterns are hung for decoration, floated on water, or released into the sky. Performers dressed as lions and dragons dance to scare away evil spirits and bring good luck. One of the most famous of these dances is Hong Kong's Fire Dragon Dance.

HALLOWEEN

Halloween is also known as All Hallows' Eve. It is the night before All Hallows' Day, a Christian festival to remember the dead. Tradition states that, for this night only, the ghosts of the dead return to our world. There are plenty of ghosts at Halloween, but they are people dressed up for fun!

Halloween is a time for bonfires, scary movies, haunted houses, and pumpkins. Children dress up in costumes to go trick-or-treating. They knock on doors asking for a treat, and if they don't get one, they perform a trick.

Apple bobbing is a Halloween game in which children try to pick up apples from a bowl of water without using their hands. They usually end up getting very wet! Pumpkins are carved with weird and wonderful faces. Candles are put inside to turn them into lanterns to ward off evil spirits.

Other countries have similar festivals to celebrate their dead. In China, they celebrate the Feast of the Hungry Ghosts. People light bonfires and lanterns to show the spirits the way back to their families.

DAY OF THE DEAD

The Mexican festival the Day of the Dead is held over two days at the beginning of November. The spirits, or ghosts, of children are believed to return to their families on the first day, and the spirits of adults return on the second day.

People pray to the spirits for good luck. They set up altars (raised platforms) in their homes or on the graves of their loved ones. They decorate the altars with candles, marigold flowers, and gifts. These items welcome those who have died back to the land of the living for a day.

Lots of food is put out for the spirits. A special bread called *pan de muerto*, which is shaped like a skull and bones, is made for the Day of the Dead. Small, brightly colored sugar skulls are also used as decorations at the festival.

On the streets, there are parades and exciting parties with singing and dancing. People dress up in skeleton costumes and paint skulls on their faces. Some wear shells that rattle on their clothes or use other noisy things to wake up the dead.

DIWALI

Diwali is the Hindu festival of lights. It is held to celebrate the victory of light over darkness and to honor the goddess of wealth, Lakshmi. It is also connected to many historic Hindu events, such as the heroic deeds of Lord Rama and the defeat of the demon king Ravana. Sikhs and Jains also celebrate Diwali.

The word Diwali means "rows of lights." On the night of the new moon, homes and temples are lit up with hundreds of candles and small lamps filled with oil, called *diyas*. It is hoped that the lights will encourage Lakshmi to bring good fortune.

People clean their houses and decorate the floors with beautiful patterns called *rangoli*. These patterns are made out of colored powder and often feature the lotus flower. People dress in their best clothes and pray at the temple.

It is also a time for fun. People get together with friends and family and wish them a happy Diwali. They exchange gifts and sweets called *mithai*, enjoy a special feast, and watch firework displays.

THANKSGIVING

Thanksgiving Day is celebrated mainly in the United States and Canada, where it is one of the biggest holidays of the year. People give thanks for their good fortune, and Christians say a prayer at the dinner table before enjoying a Thanksgiving feast.

The earliest Europeans to settle (live) in what would become the United States and Canada held celebrations to show their thanks for good harvests and good fortune. In 1621, European settlers in New England shared their Thanksgiving feast with the Native Americans who had helped them survive their first year living there.

Thanksgiving dinner includes such dishes as turkey with stuffing, mashed potatoes, beans, corn, and pumpkin or apple pie. Each year, the president of the United States saves, or "pardons," one or two turkeys from being eaten.

On Thanksgiving, people often watch football games, and in the United States, people go to parades where giant balloons float above the crowds. The most famous parade is the Macy's Thanksgiving Day Parade in New York, which is one of the biggest parades in the world.

INTERNATIONAL FESTIVAL OF THE SAHARA

This festival is held in Douz, a small town on the edge of the Sahara Desert in Tunisia. It began as a camel festival and has since become a celebration of the culture and traditions of North Africa. Desert people gather together to teach others about their way of life.

A grand parade marks the beginning of four days of events. These include camel, horse, and dog races. There are performances about desert life and games of sand hockey. In the grand finale of the parade, stunt riders jump onto galloping horses and attempt daring balancing acts.

Traditional music and dance displays feature artists in beautiful costumes. Many dances are performed, including a Berber dance, in which women twirl their brightly colored skirts and flick their hair in time to a drum beat. Belly dancers and acrobats also demonstrate their skills.

In the town of Douz, a huge market sells local goods, such as dates. Visitors enjoy food cooked over open fires, including a stuffed bread known as Berber pizza. They may attend craft shows, art performances, and poetry competitions.

43

GROUNDHOG DAY

Groundhog Day in the United States and Canada celebrates a superstition that if a groundhog (a squirrel-like animal) comes out of its burrow on February 2 and sees its shadow, winter will continue for another six weeks. If the weather is cloudy, so there is no shadow, people believe that spring will arrive early.

HANUKKAH

Hanukkah is the Jewish festival of lights. It marks the remembrance of the victory of the Jews against the Greeks, who had banned Jewish worship. The Jews got their holy temple back and lit an oil lamp with enough oil for just one day. Amazingly, the lamp burned for eight days, so Hanukkah lasts this long.

DONGJI

Dongji is the Korean festival of midwinter. People make a special red bean porridge with small balls of rice in it called *patjuk*. It is thought that the red beans protect against evil spirits and bad luck, while the rice symbolizes new life.

ANZAC DAY

Anzac Day honors soldiers from Australia and New Zealand who died in past battles. It is held on April 25, the anniversary of a battle in 1915, the first of World War I in which soldiers from these countries fought. The day is marked with prayers, laying of wreaths, and the playing of national anthems.

THE CHRISTMAS SEASON

The figure of Santa Claus can be traced back to Saint Nicholas, from the fourth century. His feast day is celebrated in many European countries on December 5–6. Children leave a special boot out for Saint Nicholas to fill with gifts if they have been good.

In many places, people exchange gifts and enjoy a festive meal on December 24, known as Christmas Eve. A midnight church service is held to mark the birth of Jesus Christ. Christmas trees are decorated with ornaments and lights, and homes are adorned with tinsel.

Three Kings' Day, on January 6, celebrates the day that three kings visited the baby Jesus. In Spanish-speaking countries, crown-shaped pastries called rosca de reyes, or king's cake, are eaten, and children polish their boots so they can be filled with presents.

December 25 is Christmas Day! In the United States, people exchange presents and eat dishes such as turkey, ham, mashed potatoes, pie, and fruitcake. Children leap out of bed early to see if Santa Claus has come down the chimney and left gifts under the Christmas tree.

KATY HALFORD

Katy Halford is an illustrator based in Leicestershire in the UK. Her love of drawing started when she was small and continued all the way through school and college. She graduated from Loughborough University with a degree in illustration and is now a full-time illustrator.

Katy's work always starts in her sketchbook, where she dreams up colorful characters and imaginary worlds. Observing nature and people watching are Katy's favorite things to do to get inspiration—she's always looking for ideas in the everyday world.

Her amazing artworks are mostly digital, but from time to time she creates and scans patterns and textures to use in her work.